Dedicated to
my superhero parents
Zelime ("Tootsie") and Hank ("Colonel")
and to The Amen Family Band

Dad (Hank), Zelime, Barbara, Henry, Mom (Zelime),
Lucy, Beth, Ruth, Nelson

"Music is beautiful, dazzling,
and remarkable!"

- Third Grade Student

Copyright © 2018
Written by Lucy A. Warner
Illustrated by Patrick Ackerman
Designed by Jaclyn Alvarado

Editorial Staff:
Dr. Patricia A. Flynn
Laura Muhlfeld
Nicholas Warner

ISBN 978-0-692-10780-5

Spring Promise Productions LLC
PO Box 558
New York, NY 10021
SpringPromiseProductions@gmail.com
www.SpringPromiseProductions.com

Printed in the United States of America.
Signature Book Printing, www.sbpbooks.com

ZAP! BAM! NOW!
SUPERHEROES OF MUSIC

Twelve Famous Composers with Super Powers!

Written by Lucy A. Warner, M.A.

Illustrated by Patrick Ackerman

DEAR READER

Everyone loves a superhero. Well, almost everyone!

What if famous musicians from long ago were really superheroes? What would each one's special power be? In this second book of the ZAP! series, you'll learn some interesting facts about twelve more composers. You'll discover a wonderful piece of music each one composed - and what he or she might have looked like as a superhero!

Inspired by my students, this book is meant for children. Adults are invited, too! Why? Because experiencing music is a fantastic adventure for everyone!

LUCY A. WARNER

TABLE OF CONTENTS...

FRANCESCA CACCINI – "ZAP!"

Francesca (frahn-chess-kah) Caccini (Kah-chee-nee) (1587-1641) of Italy grew up in a musical family. Caccini was an excellent singer. She also played several instruments, including the lute, which is a pear-shaped, stringed instrument related to the guitar.

Do you know how many strings a lute has? The number of strings on different types of lutes varies – from around eight to as many as twenty-eight! A **lutenist** needs to make sure all the strings are correctly **tuned**, so that the instrument will sound its very best.

Francesca Caccini became a highly regarded music instructor of princesses and other royalty in the city of Florence. She was well paid by the Medici (med-dee-chee) Court to compose instrumental and vocal music. This was remarkable because, during that time in history, women were not usually allowed to have a career writing music. This type of work was reserved for men. Besides being an accomplished singer and lutenist, Caccini was the first woman to write an **opera**!

What if Caccini were a superhero with a magical, 15-stringed lute? Dancing in the sky, she could charge her fantastic hands to send powerful, musical, electric shocks – "Zap!" All the strings on her amazing lute would tune themselves!

What beautiful sounds the lute can bring
While dancers dance and singers sing.
Composed back then, now musicians play
Wonderful works from that bygone day.

Great music was written by men, it's true.
And women? Oh! Could they compose, too?
The answer is "Yes," as you will see
When you listen to Francesca Caccini.

LISTEN TO CACCINI!

Ciaccona

GIOACHINO ROSSINI – "ZING!"

Gioachino (jee-ah-kee-no) Rossini (roh-see-nee) (1792-1868) was born in Italy. His father played the trumpet, and his mother was an excellent singer. When Gioachino was only six years old, he played the **triangle** in his dad's band!

Rossini is best known for composing **operas**. In the opening of an opera, before the action begins onstage, the **orchestra** plays music which "sets the mood" for the drama. This type of instrumental **composition** is called an **overture**.

The most famous overture written by Rossini is from his opera *William Tell*. The music has a part for the triangle to play! This opera tells the story of a legendary Swiss hero named William Tell. One day, a cruel governor commanded Tell's son to stand with an apple on his head, far away from his father. Then, Tell was given one chance to aim the arrow in his bow and shoot the apple off the boy's head. If Tell failed, both would be put to death. Tell was a skilled marksman. He succeeded. Their lives were saved!

What if Rossini were a fantastic, flying archer with a magical triangle and a special apple that could stay suspended in the air? Then, Super Rossini could whisk through the sky, shoot the arrow perfectly through the triangle, and split the apple - "Zing!"

Aim it well,
William Tell
Save your son
With just one

Shot of the arrow
Strong and narrow.
The apple's split -
A perfect hit!

LISTEN TO ROSSINI!

William Tell Overture
from *Guillame Tell*

LOUISE FARRENC — "ZONK!"

Louise Farrenc (fah-rawnk) (1804-1875) was a French pianist and **composer**. When Louise was a little girl, her last name was Dumont (dew-maw). Many members of her family were famous sculptors and painters. They encouraged Louise to develop her creative talents, including composing music.

Farrenc became a renowned piano teacher at the prestigious Paris Conservatory. For many years, she was the school's only woman professor! She also performed concerts and wrote **symphonies** and **chamber works**. Usually, only men were encouraged and allowed to compose. Farrenc was very humble and did not brag about her incredible, musical accomplishments. Her husband realized her greatness, and he convinced her to keep writing music. He helped make her music known to many people.

Do you know what a **nonet** (no-net) is? It is a piece written for nine instruments. Farrenc achieved great fame for her *Nonet*. Because of this composition, her boss at the Paris Conservatory finally agreed to pay her the same salary as the male professors!

What if Farrenc had super-powered laser eyes that could suddenly create a fantastic, musical sculpture of the nine instruments that play in her *Nonet*? "Zonk!"

Oboe, clarinet, bassoon, French horn
Plus flute, four strings - a nonet is born.
Who wrote this piece, the first of its kind,
A woman? It's true - a musical "find!"

Make room for her talents on history's pages
No longer forgotten in schools and on stages.
Bells should ring and horns should honk
For this great woman - Louise Farrenc!

LISTEN TO FARRENC!

Nonet, Op. 38
Third Movement

FRÉDÉRIC CHOPIN – "TRILL!"

Frédéric (fred-rick) Chopin (show-pan) (1810-1849) is Poland's most famous composer. He grew up with three sisters. As a young boy, he loved music, art, and poetry. He wrote his first musical piece when he was only seven years old! Chopin became a **virtuoso** pianist and popular **composer**. He is often called the "Poet of the Piano." His works are for solo piano or piano with other instruments.

Do you know what a **nocturne** (nahk-turn) is? A nocturne is a musical piece with a beautiful, **lyrical melody**. Chopin composed twenty-one of these types of pieces for piano! Chopin's nocturnes sound dreamy, sometimes a bit sad. In his Nocturne No. 20, you can hear two notes that are very close in **pitch** being played back and forth extremely fast - a musical ornament called a **trill**. Chopin used trills to make his melodies sound even more expressive. He dedicated Nocturne No. 20 to his beloved, older sister Ludwika (lood-vee-kuh).

One evening, during a fierce thunderstorm, Chopin was inside practicing piano. Lost in the melody, he imagined that he was a heavenly "Protector of the Piano" superhero, with amazingly powerful, musical breath. As Chopin was flying and floating up, up into the dark, rain-battered sky, the water was not able to touch him or his piano! And each time there was a trill in the music, the warm breath coming out of Chopin's mouth magically found the two notes - and played them. "Trill!"

A two-note trill
A beautiful thrill
His melodious art
Touches the heart.

Chopin could write
Of darkness and light
Sensitive, bold -
Musical gold!

LISTEN TO CHOPIN!

Nocturne No. 20
in C# minor

ROBERT SCHUMANN – "DREAM!"

Robert Schumann (shoo-mahn) (1810-1856), from Germany, started piano lessons when he was seven. As a child and as an adult, he composed music and wrote poems.

Schumann married a young woman named Clara. She was a brilliant, renowned concert pianist. She was also a **composer**. Robert and Clara raised seven children. Robert Schumann was a loving father. He enjoyed playing with his sons and daughters. He took them on walks and on other outdoor adventures. Often, he felt like a child himself!

Robert Schumann's musical works include **symphonies**, songs, and music for **solo** piano. He wrote a beautiful, engaging collection of thirteen short piano pieces. It is called *Kinderszenen* (kinn-duhr-tsay-nenn), which means *Scenes from Childhood*. Each section musically describes an event from youth.

The most famous *Kinderszenen* piece is *Träumerei* (troy-meh-rye) or *Dreaming*. It describes a child daydreaming peacefully, enjoying pleasant thoughts.

One chilly afternoon, relaxing by the fire, Schumann daydreamed that he had the super power to see - and actually relive - a childhood memory! He traveled back, back, back in time until he was a boy again, happily riding his hobbyhorse. "Dream!"

Sitting by the fireplace
Feeling music's warm embrace
What new melodies would he find
As childhood memories crossed his mind?

The flowing sounds of *Träumerei*
Bring glowing thoughts of days gone by.
Robert Schumann wrote with his heart.
He gave us beauty; he gave us art!

LISTEN TO SCHUMANN!

"Träumerei" ("Dreaming") from *Kinderszenen* (*Scenes from Childhood*)

RICHARD WAGNER - "CRASH!"

Richard Wagner (ree-khard vahg-nair) (1813 – 1883), from Germany, is famous for his **operas**. Unlike most other opera **composers**, Wagner insisted on writing the **libretto** (lih-bret-toe), or words, in addition to the music.

The opera *Die Walküre* (dee val-kyr-uh) features nine super-powered maiden-warriors or Valkyries (vahl-keer-eez). In this story, the Valkyries rush through the sky on flying horses during a ferocious battle. They circle the battlefield below, swooping down to collect fallen heroes. Then, the riders gallop at top speed, up, up, higher and higher! They whisk away the dead soldiers to the mythical Great Hall, where the heroes will join the gods at a magnificent feast in the heavens.

Wagner loved the powerful sounds of trumpets, trombones, French horns, and tubas. He even invented a new instrument called the **Wagner Tuba**. In the Ride of the Valkyries, listen to the **brass** instruments! You can also hear the **cymbals** (sim-bulls) play seventeen times!

What if Wagner had the super power to join the Valkyries and gallop across the sky on a magical Tuba Horse, surrounded by flying cymbals? "Crash!"

Ride, ride across the sky
Cymbals crash, horses fly!
Women warriors numbering nine
Race and chase on a mission divine.

Powerful sounds thrill the hall
Brass, with tuba, sound the call.
Music, drama, fantasy, glory
That's how Wagner told the story.

LISTEN TO WAGNER!

"Ride of the Valkyries"
from *Die Walküre*,
Third Act

JOHANNES BRAHMS – "WHOOSH!"

Johannes (yo-ha-ness) Brahms (brahmz) (1833-1897) was born in Germany. When he was only twelve years old, Brahms wrote a type of piece called a **sonata (so-nah-tah)**. After he finished playing this on the piano, Brahms realized how much he enjoyed composing!

Brahms loved to walk in the forest, hands behind his back, listening to the sounds of nature. Sometimes he would hike along trails in famous mountains known as the Alps.

Brahms wrote four **symphonies**. In the first **movement** of Symphony No. 4, violins play two-note patterns which move down, then up, down, then up. As the **melody** continues, the first pair of notes starts with a sigh followed by an upward glide. One afternoon, after writing this music, Brahms put down his pen. He sat back in his chair. As he stared out his window at the beautiful Alps, he started humming. He daydreamed that he had super-powered feet which made it possible for him to float across the mountain air. Now, he was suspended above the paths by this melody he had just composed! The brisk wind swirled refreshingly through his beard. The energy of each two-note phrase magically propelled his feet and body forward, first downhill, then uphill, on and on with the music, until he reached home – "Whoosh! "

In the forest, walking 'round
Brahms heard Mother Nature's sound.
Smiling, he said, "Hello, trees!"
Then he wrote some melodies.

Symphonies, piano music, songs, and more
Brahms worked hard on each musical score.
He grew a beard quite thick and wide
And kept it till the day he died.

LISTEN TO BRAHMS!

Symphony No. 4, Op. 98, First Movement

CAMILLE SAINT-SAËNS – "GLIDE!"

Camille (keh-mee-yuh) Saint-Saëns (seh-sawss) (1835-1921) was born in Paris, France. By the time he was three, he could play tunes on the piano "by ear." He became an excellent pianist and organist. Camille did a good job studying in school. He also enjoyed learning about stars and planets.

One of Saint-Saëns's most popular musical works is called *The Carnival of the Animals*. This is a **suite** of fourteen sections or **movements**. Saint-Saëns had a lot of fun writing *Carnival*! He composed it to help his students learn more about the orchestra. Using different instruments and melodies, he described various animals, such as lions and kangaroos. Towards the end of *Carnival*, you can even hear the distinctive "hee-haw!" sounds of donkeys laughing!

The most famous animal in *Carnival* is the swan. With the rich, soulful sounds of the cello, we can imagine a beautiful swan swimming smoothly across a lake.

One night, after he finished writing the swan's melody, Saint-Saëns dreamed that he was a superhero descendant of King Neptune, the ancient Roman God of Water. Swirling and whirling gently in the lake, the composer commanded his cello trident's musical notes to help him ride the swan – "Glide!"

He rises from the deep, water-soaked land,
A cello trident in his hand.
Its strings come to life as he rides on
The melody of the graceful swan.

Animals parade along the shore
Kangaroos jump and lions roar.
Of all this music, he's the boss
Now children know Camille Saint-Saëns.

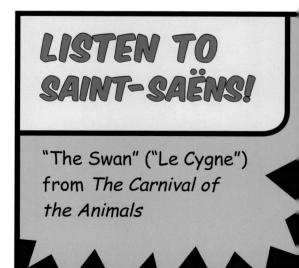

LISTEN TO SAINT-SAËNS!

"The Swan" ("Le Cygne") from *The Carnival of the Animals*

CLAUDE DEBUSSY – "SWISH!"

As a youth, **Claude (clawed) Debussy (deb-yew-see) (1862-1918)** of France showed great musical talent. Although his family was poor, he attended a famous music school. He became an excellent pianist! When Debussy was a young man, a wealthy Russian woman hired him for three summers to play piano **duets** and teach her children. Debussy's life was filled with fine things, and he was invited to beautiful, large homes and palaces. These experiences were in stark contrast to those of his childhood.

Debussy had creative ideas. He wanted to write new music that was different and fresh. His **symphonic poem** called *Prelude to the Afternoon of a Faun* has flowing shades of sounds melting into each other, depicting dreamlike scenes, with bursts of musical color. This piece was inspired by a poem about a faun - a half-man, half-goat creature popular in Greek mythology. This musical story was also performed as a **ballet**.

Debussy's *Prelude* begins with a **solo** flute melody. Then, **harps** and other instruments join in, as we imagine the mythical faun, happy in its natural setting.

One day, Debussy daydreamed that he was a Super Shepherd Genie with special powers. He was inside a magical flute, waiting to come out and enjoy the afternoon. The flute played its melody, and – "Swish!" Debussy appeared!

Claude Debussy made quite an impression
With every performance and musical session.
He painted images with novel sounds
He stretched tradition by leaps and bounds.

His music about a mythical creature
Was also praised as a ballet feature.
Listen and see the faun dance with delight
As the music caresses your dreams tonight.

LISTEN TO DEBUSSY!

Prelude to the
Afternoon of a Faun

SCOTT JOPLIN – "BAM!"

American composer **Scott Joplin (1868-1917)** was born near the Texas-Arkansas state line, just outside the city of Texarkana. Joplin's home was filled with musical sounds! His father played the fiddle (violin). His mother played the **banjo**. When he was a young boy, Joplin learned to play the banjo and the piano.

Have you ever heard of **ragtime**? In a ragtime piece, or "rag," for **solo** piano, the left hand keeps a steady beat with a repeating "boom-chick" pattern – a low-**pitched** note or **octave** followed by a **chord**. The right hand plays the **melody** with jazzy **syncopation** and a bouncy feel. Joplin is known as the "King of Ragtime" because he was such a fantastic ragtime piano player, and because he composed a large number of well-written rags. His two most famous are *The Entertainer* and *Maple Leaf Rag*.

Joplin also wrote two **operas**. One was lost and has never been found. His other one, named *Treemonisha* (tree-moh-nish-uh), is known as the first American opera!

Once, as soon as Joplin finished playing *The Entertainer*, he smiled and exclaimed, "Oh, yeah – Bam!" Was this a superhero command? What if the word "Bam!" transformed his piano into a magical, flying carpet! Joplin could fly anywhere he wanted to go!

Black keys, white keys, musical tag
Notes chase and step – it's a Joplin rag!
The left hand walks with steady feet
The right hand dances to a syncopated beat.

From classical opera to ragtime ambition
Joplin became a great musician.
How would you like to take some rides
On the flying carpet that Joplin guides?

LISTEN TO JOPLIN!

The Entertainer

 .C. HANDY — "BLUES!"

William Christopher (W.C.) Handy (1873 – 1958) was born in Alabama. He and his family lived in a log cabin built by his grandfather. William studied music and learned to play the **cornet**. When he grew up, Handy became a bandleader and traveled many places, playing American **folk songs** and other popular tunes with musical **ensembles**.

One day, as Handy was standing outside the station waiting for a train, he heard a guitarist playing distinctive, soulful sounds. He wanted to learn more about this music! He discovered it had developed out of African American work songs. From that day on, Handy – an educated musician - started a list of these types of songs and wrote them down as he heard them on his travels. He even started composing his own. Handy helped make this style of Southern music called the **blues** popular all across the U.S. He is known as the "Father of the Blues." His song "St. Louis Blues" has been performed by many famous musicians, such as guitarist Django Rheinhardt, singers Bessie Smith, Billie Holiday, and Ella Fitzgerald, and trumpet player/singer Louis Armstrong.

What if Handy were a musical superhero playing a magical cornet? His sounds could create the shapes of fantastic musicians performing the "St. Louis Blues!"

A humble start,
He stands apart.
His African roots
Brought musical fruits.

He spread the news
About the blues.
The great W.C.
Made history!

LISTEN TO HANDY!

"St. Louis Blues"

IGOR STRAVINSKY – "NOW!"

Igor (ee-gohr) Stravinsky (struh-vinn-ski) (1882-1971) was born in Russia. His father was a respected **opera** singer. His mother was an accomplished pianist. Igor learned to play the piano.

Igor Stravinsky composed a famous **ballet** about a prince named Ivan and a magical, beautiful, bright-red bird – *The Firebird*. In this fairytale, Prince Ivan is hunting in the forest. He catches the Firebird, but then he sets it free. In gratitude, the Firebird gives Prince Ivan a glowing feather, telling him that, if he is ever in danger, he should flash the feather towards the sky. One day, Ivan wanders into the enchanted garden of an evil wizard named King Kastchei (kahst-cheye). The king commands his army of fighting mini-monsters to capture the prince. Just in time, Ivan remembers the special feather! He waves it high in the air. The Firebird zooms into view! It casts a spell so that Kastchei and his goblins dance furiously, faster and faster, until they fall down from exhaustion, into a deep sleep. The Firebird performs a lullaby and then flies off in an amazing flash of light. King Kastchei and his monsters disappear forever. Prince Ivan is safe and happy!

One night, Stravinsky dreamed that he possessed the Firebird's magic. Stravinsky "powered up" and swooped down just in time to rescue Prince Ivan – "Now!"

He felt music from his head to his toes
He could play piano, conduct, and compose.
He unlocked new sounds with magical keys
With brave, fresh rhythms and harmonies.

Now dancers dance while musicians play
The exciting music of his first ballet.
The Firebird's story is wonderfully told
In Stravinsky's music – so bright, so bold!

LISTEN TO STRAVINSKY!

"Infernal Dance of King Kastchei" from *The Firebird*

GLOSSARY

Ballet (bal-lay): A dance form with a history of precise steps and artistic movements, performed to music. (Examples: Stravinsky's *Firebird* and Debussy's *Prelude to the Afternoon of a Faun.*)

Banjo (bann-joh): A stringed musical instrument with a fairly long, thin neck and round body.

Blues (blooz): A type of American music with roots in African American work songs. Basic blues features a specific three-chord pattern. (Example: W.C. Handy's "St. Louis Blues.")

Brass (brass): In a standard classical orchestra, the family of instruments which features trumpet, French horn, trombone, tuba, and sometimes the Wagner tuba.

Chamber works (chaym-brr works): Musical compositions for a fairly small group of musicians, traditionally featuring one instrument per part.

Chord (kord): Two or more musical pitches sounded at the same time.

Composer (kum-poh-zer): A person who writes musical pieces.

Composition (kahm-puh-zih-shunn): A musical work or piece for instruments or voices or both.

Cornet (kor-net): A brass instrument that is very similar to the trumpet.

Cymbals (sim-bulls): Round, metal, percussive instruments that can be played alone with a mallet or stick, or as a pair, with one cymbal crashing against the other.

Duet (do-ett): A musical composition for two performers. A piano duet features two people playing different but related parts on one piano.

Ensemble (awn-sawm-bull): A group of musicians who sing or play together as a unified entity.

Folk Song (foke-sawng): A song from a particular culture or region that has been passed down through generations through oral tradition. Some songs written in that style today are also called folk songs.

Harp (harp): A musical, stringed instrument. In a standard classical orchestra, harps are very large. They have almost fifty strings.

Libretto (lih-bret-oh): The words or text for a large musical work such as an opera.

Lute (loot): A stringed instrument related to the guitar. The body of a lute usually looks like a pear-shaped bowl. Lutes vary in size. They can have several or many strings.

Lutenist (loo-tuh-nisst): A person who plays the lute.

Lyrical (lear-uh-kull): Smooth, flowing. The tempo or speed of a lyrical melody is usually medium or slow.

Melody (mel-oh-dee): The collection of musical pitches played one by one, in the order selected by the performer or the composer. The melody helps give a musical work its shape and direction, as we listen to the melody and follow it from beginning to end.

Movement (move-mint): One section of a musical work such as a symphony, concerto, or sonata. The abbreviation for "movement" is "mvt."

Nocturne (nahk-turn): A fairly short musical piece, originally for piano, with a pensive, lyrical melody. (Example: Chopin's *Nocturne No. 20 in C# minor*.)

Nonet (no-net): A musical piece for nine instruments, such as *Nonet* by F. Caccini.

Octave: Two pitches that, within the context of a diatonic scale, are eight notes apart. These two pitches have the same musical letter name.

Opera (op-purr-uh): A musical drama featuring singers accompanied by an orchestra. Operas are staged performances which include sets and costumes.

Orchestra (or-keh-struh): A group of musicians who perform as an ensemble. In a standard classical orchestra, there are four families of instruments: strings, woodwinds, brass, and percussion.

Overture (oh-ver-cherr): The opening instrumental music of an opera or other large-scale composition. An overture can also be written as an independent, complete work.

Percussion (purr-kuh-shun): In a standard classical orchestra, the family of instruments which includes the triangle, cymbals, timpani (also called kettle drums), xylophone, castanets, snare drum, and many other rhythm instruments.

Pitch (pitch): A specific sound that identifies a musical note. Big musical instruments can play low-pitched notes. Small musical instruments can play high-pitched notes.

Prelude (prell-yood): An introductory musical piece which precedes another type of composition, such as found in the music of J.S. Bach. The preludes of Chopin and Debussy stand alone as complete, independent pieces.

Ragtime (rag-time): A type of American music originally written for piano, featuring a steady rhythm in the left hand with syncopated melodies in the right hand.

Solo (so-lo): A musical piece or section of a piece for one instrument or singer performing alone, or as the featured musician in an ensemble.

Sonata (soh-nah-tuh): A type of musical piece for one or more instruments. A sonata has varied sections (movements), each with a different character or "feel."

Strings (stringz): In a standard classical orchestra, the family of instruments which features violin, viola, cello, and double bass. Some other "string" instruments are the harp and guitar. The piano belongs to the string family and to the percussion family.

Suite (sweet): In music, a suite is a collection of pieces which are played in a certain order and which together form one musical composition. (Example: Saint-Saëns's *Carnival of the Animals*.)

Symphonic poem (sim-fah-nik poh-uhm): A type of musical piece, usually in one movement, that describes or generally reflects a work of art such as a painting, poem, etc. A symphonic poem is also called a tone poem.

Symphony (sim-fuh-nee): A musical piece written for orchestra, usually with four different sections (movements).

Syncopation (sinn-koh-pay-shun): The placement of accents on beats that normally would not be the strong beats of a measure. Syncopation gives music a "jazzy" and exciting effect. Scott Joplin's piano rags feature syncopation.

Triangle (try-ang-gull): A metal, triangular-shaped percussive instrument with a clear, ringing sound. A triangle is played by striking it with a metal stick.

Trill (trill): Two notes close in pitch played very quickly back and forth, one at a time, for expressive purposes.

Tuned (toond): Set to the correct musical pitch or pitches.

Virtuoso (vurr-choo-oh-so): A singer or instrumentalist who performs with amazing skill and technique.

Wagner tuba (vahg-nair too-buh): A brass instrument invented by Richard Wagner. The Wagner tuba is a combination of French horn and trombone.

Woodwinds (wood-windz): In a standard classical orchestra, the family of instruments featuring flute, piccolo, oboe, English horn, clarinet, bass clarinet, bassoon, and contrabassoon.

MUSICAL INSTRUMENTS

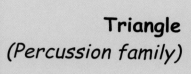

Triangle
(Percussion family)

Tuba
(Brass Family)

Flute
(Woodwind family)

Piano
(String and Percussion family)

Cello
(String family)

COMPOSER TIMELINE

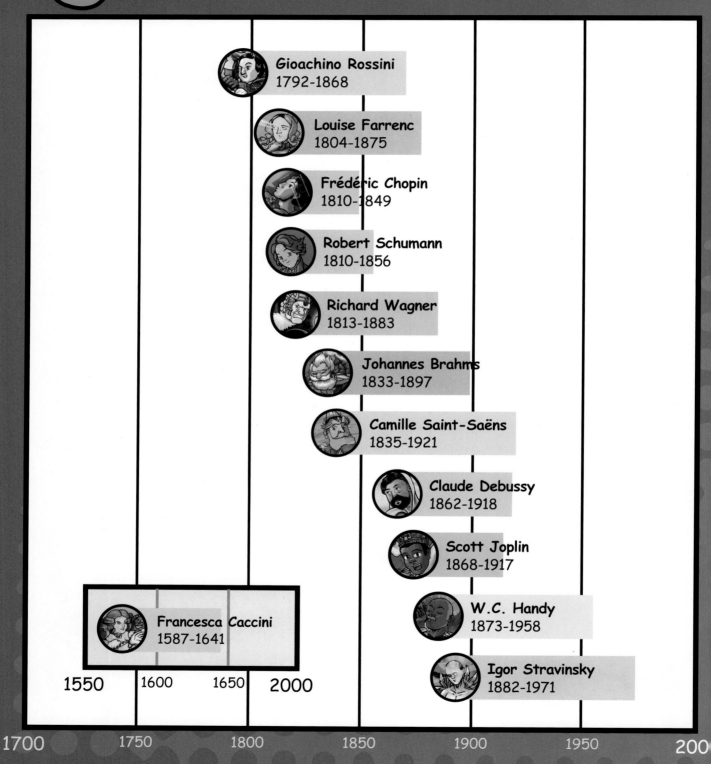

Gioachino Rossini
1792-1868

Louise Farrenc
1804-1875

Frédéric Chopin
1810-1849

Robert Schumann
1810-1856

Richard Wagner
1813-1883

Johannes Brahms
1833-1897

Camille Saint-Saëns
1835-1921

Claude Debussy
1862-1918

Scott Joplin
1868-1917

W.C. Handy
1873-1958

Francesca Caccini
1587-1641

Igor Stravinsky
1882-1971

1550   1600   1650   2000

1700   1750   1800   1850   1900   1950   200

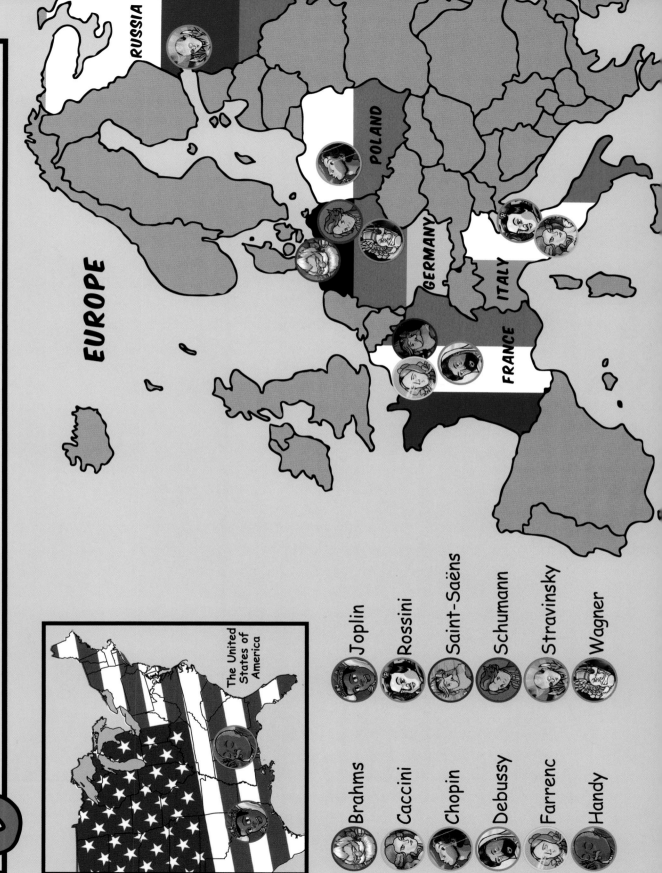

COMPOSER MAP

RUSSIA

POLAND

GERMANY

ITALY

FRANCE

EUROPE

The United States of America

Joplin

Rossini

Saint-Saëns

Schumann

Stravinsky

Wagner

Brahms

Caccini

Chopin

Debussy

Farrenc

Handy

OMPOSER QUOTES

"Without craftsmanship, inspiration is a mere reed shaken in the wind."

- BRAHMS

"Happiness is an attitude. We either make ourselves miserable, or happy and strong. The amount of work is the same."

- CACCINI

"Put all your soul into it; play the way you feel!"

- CHOPIN

"Works of art make rules; rules do not make works of art."

- DEBUSSY

"If any woman deserves to be recognized as the greatest female composer of the nineteenth century, it's Louise Farrenc."

- ABOUT FARRENC
Jerry Dubins, Fanfare, Nov/Dec 2009

"Life is something like a trumpet. If you don't put anything into it, you won't get anything out."

- HANDY

"Don't play this piece fast. It is never right to play ragtime fast."

– JOPLIN

"Give me a laundry list and I'll set it to music."

– ROSSINI

"I like good company, but I like hard work still better."

– SAINT-SAËNS

"To send light into the darkness of men's hearts – such is the duty of the artist."

– SCHUMANN

"My music is best understood by children and animals."

– STRAVINSKY

"The oldest, truest, most beautiful organ of music . . . is the human voice."

– WAGNER

QUESTIONS

1. Who is called the "Poet of the Piano?"

2. In *The Carnival of the Animals*, which instrument did Camille Saint-Saëns use to portray the swan?

3. Which composer was the first woman to write an opera?

4. How many cymbal crashes are there in Richard Wagner's *Ride of the Valkyries*?

5. Who is called the "King of Ragtime?"

6. How many symphonies did Johannes Brahms write?

7. What is the name of Louise Farrenc's composition that helped her boss realize she should be paid as much as the male professors at the Paris Conservatory?

8. What is the name of Igor Stravinsky's ballet about a prince and a magical, flying creature?

9. Is Rossini best known for his operas, piano pieces, or symphonies?

10. Who is called the "Father of the Blues?"

11. Which instrument of the orchestra plays solo at the very beginning of Claude Debussy's *Prelude to the Afternoon of a Faun*?

12. Robert Schumann's thirteen short pieces in *Scenes from Childhood* are written for what instrument?

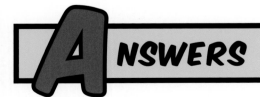

ANSWERS

1. Chopin 2. Cello 3. Francesca Caccini 4. Seventeen 5. Scott Joplin 6. Four 7. Nonet 8. *The Firebird* 9. Operas 10. W.C. Handy 11. Flute 12. Piano

LISTENING/VIEWING GUIDE

CACCINI (p. 6) - Ciaccona
https://www.youtube.com/watch?v=ja7ugHH8DtM
https://www.youtube.com/watch?v=DmHhvpbxoNM

ROSSINI (p. 8) – "William Tell Overture" from
Guillame Tell
https://www.youtube.com/watch?v=YIbYCOiETx0
https://www.youtube.com/watch?v=Kz_H8cMjBQM
[start 11:16]

FARRENC (p. 10) – Nonet Op. 38, Third Movement
https://www.youtube.com/
watch?v=kTDfDPMRUmU&list=RDkTDfDPMRUmU
https://www.youtube.com/watch?v=jvOnI9STNK8

CHOPIN (p. 12) – Nocturne No. 20 in C# minor
https://www.youtube.com/watch?v=n9oQEa-d5rU
https://www.youtube.com/
watch?v=jNgURCvNp3U&list=RDjNgURCvNp3U#t=6519
[start 1:49:13]

SCHUMANN (p. 14)– "Träumerei" ("Dreaming") from
Kinderszenen (Scenes from Childhood)
https://www.youtube.com/watch?v=Jgq16qX3bHY
[start 1:45]
https://www.youtube.com/watch?v=9zVQk0YviAA

WAGNER (p.16) – "Ride of the Valkyries" from
Die Walküre, Third Act

https://www.youtube.com/watch?v=xeRwBiu4wfQ
https://www.youtube.com/watch?v=P73Z6291Pt8

BRAHMS (p. 18) – Symphony No. 4, Op. 98,
First Movement
https://www.youtube.com/watch?v=6yy3eQwu63A
https://www.youtube.com/watch?v=fxsJ9qSsBpw

SAINT-SAËNS (p. 20) – "The Swan" ("Le Cygne")
from *The Carnival of the Animals*
https://www.youtube.com/watch?v=3qrKjywjo7Q
https://www.youtube.com/watch?v=xrQbERLGkQY

DEBUSSY (p. 22) – Prelude to the Afternoon of a Faun
https://www.youtube.com/watch?v=Y9iDOt2WbjY
https://www.youtube.com/watch?v=6SHBek8BONQ

JOPLIN (p. 24) – The Entertainer
https://www.youtube.com/watch?v=fPmruHc4S9Q
https://www.youtube.com/watch?v=kHtwF-gpluc

HANDY (p. 26) – "St. Louis Blues"
https://www.youtube.com/watch?v=D2TUIUwa3_o
https://www.youtube.com/watch?v=TmbQVx6SGao

STRAVINSKY (p. 28) – "Infernal Dance of King Kastchei"
from *The Firebird*
https://www.youtube.com/watch?v=6Vj8ow8iC4s
https://www.youtube.com/watch?v=S_6dPAVycw

BIBLIOGRAPHY

Ardley, Neil. *Eyewitness Music*. New York: DK Publishing, Inc., 2004. Print.

azquotes.com. Web. 2 March 2018

10bestquotes.com. Web. 16 Feb.2018

bestmusicquotes.wordpress.com. Web. 18 Feb. 2018

classicfm.com. Web. 11 Jan. 2018

Dubins, Jerry. Nov./Dec 2009. *Fanfare*. Amazon.com "Louise Farrenc: Piano Trios, Sextet" CD. Editorial Review. Web. 8 Feb. 2018

famous-quotes-and-quotations.com. Web. 26 Jan. 2018

Machlis, Joseph and Kristine Forney. *The Enjoyment of Music*. New York: Norton, 7th ed., 1995. Print.

ABOUT THE AUTHOR

Lucy A. Warner (B. M. Ed., M.A.), Chair of the Music Department at The Browning School in New York City, is a graduate of the University of Texas (Austin) and Eastman School of Music (Rochester, NY). An award-winning music teacher, she has over twenty years of experience instructing children in grades K through 4. *Zap! Bam! Now! Superheroes of Music* is her second book of the *Zap!* series, following the success of her first book *Zap! Boom! Pow! Superheroes of Music*.

Ms. Warner's *Zap!* writing journey grew out of the popularity of the Composer of the Month program which she initiated in the classroom. Seeing how children are energized as they learn about the lives and musical achievements of the world's most gifted and famous musicians – from Rossini to Bob Marley, to today's brightest stars – the author was inspired to present twelve composers – and now, in her second book, twelve more – with the same fresh, unique dimension. These incredible musicians are jolted to life – as superheroes!

Ms. Warner recommends *Zap! Boom! Pow!* and *Zap! Bam! Now!* for children, parents, teachers, all music-loving adults, and for reading to pets – including her son's curious, adorable cat Zion.

ABOUT THE ILLUSTRATOR

Patrick Ackerman is an illustrator/pixel artist from the tri-state area. When he's not making video games, he is playing them. His superpower allows his drum beat to tame wild animals, heal others' wounds, and drive evil *insane*.

Website: www.patackermanart.com
Tumblr: patattackerman.tumblr.com